DECOMPOSERS
Termites

by Trudy Becker

www.focusreaders.com

Copyright © 2025 by Focus Readers®, Mendota Heights, MN 55120. All rights reserved. No part of this book may be reproduced or utilized in any form or by any means without written permission from the publisher.

Focus Readers is distributed by North Star Editions: sales@northstareditions.com | 888-417-0195

Produced for Focus Readers by Red Line Editorial.

Photographs ©: Shutterstock Images, cover, 1, 4, 6, 8, 11, 12, 15, 16, 18, 21, 25, 26, 29; iStockphoto, 22

Library of Congress Cataloging-in-Publication Data
Names: Becker, Trudy, author.
Title: Termites / by Trudy Becker.
Description: Mendota Heights, MN: Focus Readers, [2025] | Series: Decomposers | Includes bibliographical references and indexes. | Audience: Grades 2-3
Identifiers: LCCN 2024029719 (print) | LCCN 2024029720 (ebook) | ISBN 9798889984016 (hardcover) | ISBN 9798889984290 (paperback) | ISBN 9798889984832 (pdf) | ISBN 9798889984573 (hosted ebook)
Subjects: LCSH: Termites--Juvenile literature.
Classification: LCC QL529 .B43 2025 (print) | LCC QL529 (ebook) | DDC 595.7/36--dc23/eng/20240705
LC record available at https://lccn.loc.gov/2024029719
LC ebook record available at https://lccn.loc.gov/2024029720

Printed in the United States of America
Mankato, MN
012025

About the Author

Trudy Becker lives in Minneapolis, Minnesota. She likes exploring new places and loves anything involving books.

Table of Contents

CHAPTER 1
Eating Old Wood 5

CHAPTER 2
Breaking It Down 9

THAT'S AMAZING!
Working Together 14

CHAPTER 3
Helping the Ecosystem 17

CHAPTER 4
Termites and the Future 23

Focus Questions • 28
Glossary • 30
To Learn More • 31
Index • 32

CHAPTER 1

Eating Old Wood

A termite crawls away from its **mound**. It moves across the forest floor. The termite needs to find food.

Soon, it finds a decaying log. The dead wood is falling apart.

 Termites don't sleep. They can be active all day.

Termites eat wood from the inside. They make tunnels.

So, the termite releases a smell. Other termites in the **colony** notice it. They know where to find the log. Then the termite starts eating. It takes small bites. So do the other termites. The log becomes smaller and smaller.

The termites return to their mound. Later, the termites poop out the wood. The poop joins the material on the forest floor. Then the termites go out to search for more food.

Did You Know?
Termites use their own poop to help build nests. **Bacteria** live in the poop. These tiny life-forms keep the nests clean and safe.

CHAPTER 2
Breaking It Down

Ecosystems have three groups of life-forms. One group makes its own food. Another group eats plants or animals. Decomposers make up the final group. They break down dead things.

Like all insects, a termite has six legs.

Termites are decomposers. Sometimes, they eat living things. But termites mostly consume dead material. For example, they eat rotting wood. They eat dead leaves. They even eat poop and soil. All these foods contain a material called cellulose.

Most animals don't eat these things. They can't break down cellulose. But termites can. They have **microorganisms** in their stomachs. These tiny creatures

Termites may eat cardboard or paper. These objects have lots of cellulose.

help break down the cellulose. Then termites can get energy from it.

Termites break things down all over the world. More than 3,000 kinds of termites exist. Many termites live in forest **habitats**.

Colonies have soldier termites. These large termites protect the nest.

Others live underground in the desert. Some termites even live in the wood of people's homes.

Termites are social animals. They live together in colonies. But only some of the termites in a colony search for food. Worker termites do this job. First, they find food. Then they eat it and break it down. It becomes a sugary substance. Finally, workers feed the substance to the rest of the colony.

Did You Know?
Some termite colonies are small. They may have a few thousand termites. Others are huge. They may have millions of termites.

THAT'S AMAZING!

Working Together

Termites and microorganisms are symbiotic. That means the two life-forms need each other to live. Termites' bodies give microorganisms a home. The termites give them food, too.

In return, microorganisms keep termites healthy. Without these creatures, termites could not eat dead material. The termites might starve as a result.

Termites have other symbiotic relationships, too. For example, some termites may work with fungi. The termites help grow the fungi. They raise and farm it. Then the fungi become food for the termites.

▶ **Termites only grow certain kinds of fungi. These fungi are called termite mushrooms.**

CHAPTER 3

Helping the Ecosystem

Termites break down and eat plant material to live. But this process also helps ecosystems. Without termites, many ecosystems would not survive. Dead plants would pile up. They would stay on the ground.

Termites help plants grow by tunneling. Tunnels help rain and air get into soil.

▷ **Termite poop adds nitrogen and phosphorus to soil. These nutrients help plants grow.**

That would hurt other life-forms. For example, dead material could block new plants from growing in the soil. That could make it harder for animals to find food to eat.

18

However, termites don't just take material out of the ecosystem. They recycle it. The recycled material comes from termites' poop. The poop puts **nutrients** back into the ground. It makes the soil stronger. Strong soil is richer. New living things can grow in it. The soil is also less likely to be washed away.

This recycling has a ripple effect. More plants grow. Other animals eat those growing plants. They get the food they need to survive.

Goanna lizards are an example of this process. Goannas live in the desert. They eat desert plants to live. But these plants could not grow without termites. So, termites help the whole chain of creatures survive. Their role is key to keeping the ecosystem in balance.

Did You Know?

Some termites build mounds. Others make nests underground. Nest tunnels can be hundreds of feet long.

Termite mounds can be huge. Some rise more than 30 feet (9 m) high.

CHAPTER 4
Termites and the Future

Termites help the planet in many ways. However, termites could also cause problems in the future. **Climate change** is threatening many ecosystems. Some gases are making Earth warmer.

Many termites live in tropical rainforests. These areas are warm and wet.

Most kinds of termites live in warm areas. But some colder areas are heating up. That creates more places where termites could live. Scientists think termites will move into these new areas. Over time, the area of termites' habitats could increase by 30 percent. For example, some cooler forests may warm up. Then termites may move in and change the ecosystem.

Termites in these forests could help break down dead material.

▷ **Termites could spread to more cities in the future. They could damage many people's homes.**

They may help other wildlife, too. But termites will also add carbon dioxide to the **atmosphere**. That is because forests hold a lot of carbon. Wood keeps carbon inside.

25

 Termites eat about seven times more wood in warmer places than in cooler places.

However, termites break down the wood. That lets the carbon back out.

With more termite habitats, termite colonies could break down more wood. They could do it at a higher speed, too. Termites eat food faster when living in warmer places. As a result, termites could speed up the effects of climate change.

Scientists are studying these problems. They hope to reduce the effects of climate change in the future.

Did You Know?
A colony of termites can decompose 11 pounds (5 kg) of wood in a month.

Focus Questions

Write your answers on a separate piece of paper.

1. Write a few sentences explaining how termites break down dead material.

2. What fact about termites is most interesting to you? Why?

3. What life-form do termites have a symbiotic relationship with?
- **A.** humans
- **B.** microorganisms
- **C.** trees

4. How could adding nutrients to the soil help other plants survive?
- **A.** The plants could live with few nutrients.
- **B.** The plants could die from termite poop.
- **C.** The plants could grow in more places.

5. What does **decaying** mean in this book?

*Soon, it finds a **decaying** log. The dead wood is falling apart.*

    A. healthy
    B. rotting
    C. green

6. What does **consume** mean in this book?

*Sometimes, they eat living things. But termites mostly **consume** dead material.*

    A. feed on
    B. ignore
    C. swim in

Answer key on page 32.

Glossary

atmosphere
The layers of gases that surround a planet, moon, or star.

bacteria
Tiny living things that can be either useful or harmful.

climate change
A human-caused global crisis involving long-term changes in Earth's temperature and weather patterns.

colony
A group of animals that live together.

ecosystems
The collections of living things in different natural areas.

habitats
The types of places where plants or animals normally grow or live.

microorganisms
Tiny creatures, such as bacteria, that can be seen only with microscopes.

mound
A hill or pile that termites build to live in.

nutrients
Substances that living things need to stay strong and healthy.

To Learn More

BOOKS

Brody, Walt. *How Is a Building Like a Termite Mound?: Structures Imitating Nature*. Minneapolis: Lerner Publications, 2022.

Olson, Elsie. *Animal Builder Brawl*. Minneapolis: Abdo Publishing, 2020.

Owen, Ruth. *Earth's Insects Need You!: Understand the Problems, How You Can Help, Take Action*. Minneapolis: Lerner Publications, 2024.

NOTE TO EDUCATORS

Visit **www.focusreaders.com** to find lesson plans, activities, links, and other resources related to this title.

Index

A
atmosphere, 25

B
bacteria, 7

C
cellulose, 10–11
climate change, 23–27
colonies, 6, 12–13, 26–27

D
decomposers, 9–10

E
ecosystems, 9, 17, 19–20, 23–24

F
fungi, 14

G
gases, 23
goanna lizards, 20

H
habitats, 11, 24, 26

M
microorganisms, 10–11, 14
mounds, 5, 7, 20

N
nests, 7, 20
nutrients, 19

S
soil, 10, 18–19

T
tunnels, 20

W
wood, 5, 7, 10, 12, 25–27
worker termites, 13